Inspirational Poems

BY BETTY VIRGINIA SHRADER

DORRANCE PUBLISHING CO
EST. 1920
PITTSBURGH, PENNSYLVANIA 15238

Dorrance Publishing Co
585 Alpha Drive
Pittsburgh, PA 15238
Visit our website at *www.dorrancebookstore.com*

ISBN: 979-8-88729-091-1
eISBN: 979-8-88729-591-6

Inspirational Poems

Glorious Mansions

Glorious mansions await me in that fair land
That is built by God's magnificent hands.
Jewels of priceless beauty my eyes shall behold.
When I stand before God on the streets of purest gold.
Laughter and joy shall enhance me on that day.
For my troubles and trials will all pass away.
I will hold to God's unchanging hand
Until he can take me to that Blessed Promised Land.
Glorious mansions await me dressed in bright array.
Where there remains for me just one eternal day.

God Understands

God understands our special needs when we pray.
He is there to help us as we call on him each day.
When we have problems we cannot understand,
God is always there to lend a helping hand.
God understands our fears and every little care.
He will never forsake us for he is always near.
His strength is sufficient and his grace each day is made anew.
His promises are never broken, for he is always there for you.
God understands the tears that flow from our eyes.
He knows just how we feel and the reason why we cry.
All he asks is simple faith and trust in him each day.
God understands for he is always there to guide our way.

My Sweet Mother

I can visualize her smile and her tender ways.
How my sweet mother would brighten up my days.
Sweet memories of her I ponder in my heart.
I know she loved me dearly for true love does not depart.
Mother never complained of the burden she had to bear.
For upon God, she would cast her every care.
Someday in Heaven I will see her again.
We'll stroll down the streets of gold, and I'll hold to her hand,
Oh, my sweet mother, may your memories linger near.
As I thank God for a mother who to me was so dear.

God Bless The Nurse

God Bless the nurse in a special way
As she waits on her patients from day to day.
God give her love, strength, and courage to face each day
While she's helping others mend along the way.
When you see the tears that flows from her eyes,
Let her know on You, God, is where her strength relies.
For it is only by Your grace that we are all able to stand.
Until You are ready to take us to the Blessed Promise Land.
God Bless the nurse in a special way.
May the kindness she has shown to others return to her someday.

I'M Just A Country Boy

I'm just a country boy, as you can see.
I'm not a City Slicker like some folks may be.
I love to ride my tractor through the fields every day.
My favorite jobs are plowing and putting up the hay.
I love to take my hounds coon hunting late at night.
Just to hear those dogs yelp is my delight.
Plowing up my garden is what I do in early spring.
I plant the seeds and wait to see what they will bring.
I roam the hills on a long summer day,
Trying to find the cow that lost its way.
I'm just a Country Boy as you can see.
No one will ever take the country out of me.
So I'll just keep working the fields from day to day.
I love being Country, and that's the way I want to stay.

Good-Bye, My Love, Good-Bye

Good-bye, my love, good-bye, you will be missed while you are gone.
I'll patiently watch and wait for you until you arrive safely back home.
I see you in the things I touch and in everything I do.
Your sweet memories linger with me when I think of you.
The joy you have bought to my heart may never be known.
I have loved you so much, it seemed you were my very own.
The miles may lay between us, but true love can never depart.
I'll always think about you and love you forever in my heart.
Your laughter, smiles, and gentle little ways
Will linger with me for the rest of my days.
Good-bye, my love, good-bye until I can see you again.
You were my joy, my laughter, and my very best friend.

Memories

Memories are recollections that never fade away.
Picturesque scenes of your childhood on a bright summer day.
Old scenes of the farmhouse are recalled now and then,
Where your family once lived and your childhood began.
Walking through the fields and orchards that were so grand.
Recollections of your mother holding to your hand.
Kinfolks coming to see you from far and near.
These are precious memories that to you are so dear.
When friends loved and helped each other
Are times you can recall.
Memories of your childhood when you were very small.
Although memories are recollections that will never fade away,
You can treasure them forever and cherish them each day.

Thou Art Mine

O Lord, my God, thou art mine.
A faithful friend who to me is so divine.
When I call upon Your name, You are always there
To meet my every need and answer every prayer.
A friend who stays so close by my side.
In You, Lord, only will my trust abide.
When I have a problem that I need to share,
I call upon You, Lord, for I know that you always care.
A friend that sticketh closer than a brother.
Without You, Lord, I could find none other.
A shelter from the storms of this life in You I find.
O Lord, my God, thou art mine.

Our Pastor

Our Pastor is loving and kind indeed.
A godly man who is always helping those in need.
For years we have heard him preach in a mighty way,
Telling others about God and the Great Judgement Day.
The attitude, grace, and love of this special man
Is what it takes to enter The Blessed Promised Land.
For he is just a vessel from which the word of God proceeds,
Teaching others about God and only on him to believe.
He is a shepherd who watches over his flock with care.
In the time of sickness and trouble, he has always been there.
We want to thank you, Pastor, on this special day
For the inspiration you have been to us along this way.
Today we wish only the very best for you.
May God bless you and keep you in everything you do.

Christmas

Christmas is a wonderful time of the year.

A time when our Savior was born who to us is very dear.

At Christmas let us all bow our heads and pray.

To thank God for sending Jesus on this special day.

It's not the pretty presents wrapped up in bright array.

It's a time of praise and glory to God on this day.

Christmas is a time to thank God for everything.

For the blessings he has given, I give honor to his name.

This Christmas remember what this day really means.

It's a special day to worship Jesus, our savior and coming King.

In Heaven

In Heaven is where my soul desires to be,
To reign and live with my God eternally.
I'll walk upon the streets of gold.
My eyes shall behold the sights that have never been told.
I'll get to see my Heavenly Father who watches over me,
Who gave his son, Jesus, so I could live eternally.
To thank him and praise him for what he has done.
For giving me the victory and the crown, I have won.
Troubles and trials will all pass away from me.
For in heaven, I will rest eternally.
I'll get to see my loved ones who have gone ahead of me.
In heaven with my God, my soul shall forever be.

Pastor's Day

May God bless you and your family on this day.
May God bestow blessings upon you in his own way.
For the kindness you have shown to everyone.
For the thoughtful deeds you have done.
May God render unto you a touch of his love.
And fill you with the blessings from above.
For the word of God, you have preached from day to day.
Seeking for the lost sheep that have gone astray.
May God reward you with peace from above.
May your souls bask in his wonderful love.
Today the best is wished for you,
For you have stood as soldiers brave and true
And taught us on God's word we must all stand.
Until we have reached that Blessed Promise Land.

God Is Close To Thee

There is no God as close as thee
Who could so lovingly care about me.
Sometimes I am down and in despair,
Then I whisper to My God a little prayer
Who then can help me along this way.
Guiding me safely so I won't go astray.
It's the God that I worship and adore every day.
The one who cares for me in every way.
He is the God of the universe and the one I love
Who has touched my life with strength from above.
There is no other God as close as thee.
Thou art my creator, my master, and my deity.

Each Day I Thank You

Each day I thank you for the blessings you have bestowed upon me.
For the beautiful flowers, trees, and roaring oceans that I see.
Your marvelous grace is renewed unto me each day.
And your grace is sufficient to me in every way.
O that I may magnify your name is praise
And each day thank you for changing my ways.
For you, God, are everything to me.
My master, my creator, and my deity.
Each day I thank you for standing by me.
For hearing my prayers as I cry unto thee.
On thee, My God, I shall solely stand.
And each day thank you for holding my hand.

Don't Weep For Me

Please don't weep for me, my friend.
My life here has reached its final end.
My soul has crossed that mystic sea.
Where with my God, I shall forever be.
Troubles and trials here are now passed.
I'm free, Praise God, free at last.
To see my loved ones who went ahead of me.
At last their faces I will gladly see.
God will wipe every tear from my eyes.
As to all my friends, I said my final good-bye.
Down here I served the Lord with all of my heart.
I've reached my final destination never to depart.
Don't weep for me, my friend.
My life here has just began.

Autumn

The golden trees glisten in the beautiful sun.
Bringing forth the beauty that the Lord has done.
The leaves flow gently through the air,
Falling to the ground where they will remain there.
Tiny squirrels are busy hiding their nuts beneath the ground.
For autumn will soon pass and winter will come around.
The beautiful blue skies are all aglow.
Frost has now covered the earth below.
Autumn is such a beautiful season I know.
For the beauty my eyes beholds tells me so.
Beauty in the leaves that an artist could not design.
Beauty that is yours and beauty that is mine.
Although autumn is a season that will come and go.
I know the Lord could only place this beauty here below.

Winter In West Virginia.

The lofty green mountains are laden with snow
That has fallen from above and covered them below.
Barren trees are arrayed with coats of ice.
To the eyes of the beholder, it's a beautiful sight.
The fields are covered with blankets of white.
For the snow has fallen night after night.
Tiny squirrels are hidden high in the trees in their nests,
For the deep snow has given them a little rest.
The cattle are standing still along with their calves so small.
Winter has taken hold of these mountains so tall.
It appears to be just a forest of white.
To me wintertime in West Virginia is a beautiful sight.

Time

Time has a way of passing so fast.
Where it has went is really hard to grasp.
In your youth, you feel so young and free.
As you get older, you slow down to a certain degree.
Time doesn't change the memories you hold.
They are precious to you as you grow old.
The children you held so close to your breasts
Are all grown now, and you have some time to rest.
Time has a way of healing all of our hurts.
If we look back on our life, things could have been worse.
Take time today to enjoy your life.
Forgetting about your problems, troubles, and strife.
Look up to God and thank him for his precious love.
For in time you shall reach your eternal home above.

God Bless America

God bless America, the land of the free.
Where the flag is raised high and waves vibrantly,
God bless all the soldiers who did not die in vain.
They gave their lives completely so freedom could reign.
A land where opportunity and independence is at hand.
Where freedom of speech and religion is given to every man.
We often take for granted the freedom we possess.
Without the realization that this nation is so blessed.
God bless America, the land of the free.
We give praise to God for our liberty.

Cast All Your Care Upon Me

"Cast all your care upon me," the Lord doth say.
I will help you and strengthen you from day to day.
Look up to me when burdens are hard to bear.
I can see your every need as you call on me in prayer.
"I am touched by your infirmities," the Lord doth say.
Believe in me, and I will stablish you in my own way.
Think it not strange for the fiery trails you may face.
Just trust in me, and I will give to you more grace.
Grace to stand when trials are hard to bear.
Just trust me, child, and upon me cast all of your care.

Stand Tall

When you think you are about to fall, stand tall.
Look up to God, who is the Creator of all.
There's not a problem or fear that He can't relieve.
If only on Him you will believe,
God healed the sick, the lame, and blind.
He even touched Legion who was out of his mind.
God raised the dead and parted the sea.
He can do the same for you and me.
So stand tall when you don't know what to do.
He'll give you the strength to carry you through.
God will walk with you when no one else is there,
He'll carry your burdens, sorrows, and cares.
So stand tall, my friend, stand tall.
God is willing to help you, if on Him you will call.

When Everyone Else Is Gone

When everyone else is gone, I'll be there.
To meet your needs and to answer your prayers.
I'm the God of the Universe and the God over all.
I see everything and I'm touched, even by a sparrow that falls.
So look up to me for everything you need.
I'll give you the desires of your heart, if you only believe.
I've rolled back the waters for my children in the past.
I'll do the same for you, if only you will ask.
So when everyone else is gone, look up to me.
I'll give you the strength to go on if you only believe.

Mother

A friend who is loving and kind indeed.
Someone you can talk to when you have a problem or need.
She holds you gently and rocks you to sleep.
There is no one like her for her love is very deep.
Mother teaches you to do the things that are right.
She watches over you and cares for you both day and night.
Her hands are always busy tending to all your needs.
She teaches you about God and only on him to believe.
Mother calls your name when it is time to eat.
She prays with you when it is time to go to sleep.
Mother, you are really missed today.
For the Lord has already called you away.
My love for you, Mother, will never depart.
The fond memories of you are always in my heart.
Today, if I could be a model of someone I knew.
My dear Mother, I would be just like you.

Lord, Give Me Strength To Face Each Day

Lord, give me strength to face each day.

Touch me and help me in your own way.

Lord, my pain is so hard to bear.

I just close my eyes and whisper to you a prayer.

A prayer of faith that you will touch me again.

You, Lord, are a true and faithful friend.

A friend that sticketh closer than a brother.

Without you, Lord, I can find none other.

Friends forsake me when I need someone to care.

I can call upon You, and You, Lord, are always there.

My heart desires to be in Heaven with You.

A place where I can rest when my work on earth is through.

Give me strength from day to day.

I will trust You, Lord, in my own weak way.

Trusting in You until I reach Heaven someday.

Where I'll give you praise for the strength to face each day.

The One Who Walks With Me

The one who walks with me is loving, kind, and true.
He was born of a virgin and was King of the Jews.
One touch from him, and I've never been the same.
I can call on him anytime, and Jesus is his name,
He says in his word to ask and you shall receive.
Anything in his name if you only believe.
I've walked in valleys so low and I've climbed mountains so tall.
He lifted me up and gave me the strength to go through it all.
I give praise, honor, and glory all to him.
He is a faithful friend on whom I can depend.
As I walk on through my journey here below,
I want Jesus to walk with me everywhere I go.

My Heavenly Father Cares

Whenever I have burdens, sorrows, or fears,
I go to my Heavenly Father who cares.
He is always there to meet every need.
If only on Him I will believe,
He helps me through the burdens I bear.
There's never a problem with Him I cannot share.
He touches me again and again.
I know He's a faithful friend on whom I can depend.
When I have burdens, sorrows, or fears,
I go to my Heavenly Father who cares.

Your Heavenly Father Watches

I've seen the tears in your eyes.
Your Heavenly Father watches from the skies.
He knows the burdens that you bear.
Every little sorrow and every care.
Why worry so much, my little child.
For sorrow and tears will be gone in a little while.
There's a land where there is joy and peace.
A long white table where God's children will feast.
So look up to God who is full of love,
He will touch you from above.
He'll give you the strength that you need.
If only on him you will believe.

Heaven

I often dream of Heaven and how it will be.
When I close my eyes and go to sleep and live eternally.
Heaven will be a place where I can lay my burdens down.
I'll be given a robe of white and a bright shining crown.
I can visualize a crystal river that is perfectly clear.
Standing there is my Savior, who to me is very dear.
Although it hasn't entered into my heart what my eyes shall behold.
I can just imagine those streets of purest gold.
Just to see the gates of pearl and be able to step inside.
I'll go to my Heavenly home where I'll forever abide.
Heaven will be a place where there will be no more night.
For God Himself shall reign and He shall be the light.
I want to keep on dreaming of Heaven and how it will be.
Until I reach my final goal and live eternally.

The Eternal Home Of The Soul

When my Heavenly Father calls, I want to go.

To Heaven: The eternal home of the soul.

I want to walk on streets of purest gold.

To look upon the beauty that my eyes shall behold.

My Heavenly Father will wipe the tears from my eyes.

He'll say, "Welcome home, my child, you'll never have to say goodbye."

There is such a longing in my soul to go.

For there will be no more troubles and trials here below.

I'll get to see my loved ones that have gone ahead of me.

What a happy meeting that will surely be.

By faith we will make it to that beautiful land.

Where mansions are prepared by the Heavenly Father's hands.

When my Heavenly Father calls, I want to go.

To Heaven: The eternal home of the soul.

Angels All Around

Angels seem to be all around.
On stamps, in books, and even statues of them can be found.
Even when Christ was born, the angels were near.
To bring comfort, peace, and to spread good cheer.
Angels shut the lion's mouth when Daniel was thrown into their den.
Protecting and keeping any harm from coming to him.
When the devil tempted Jesus and thought he could get him down.
Angels ministered unto him and appeared all around.
Angels watch over little children with tender care.
Protecting them from harm or danger that may be near.
I know God's angels are all around.
Even when troubles and trials try to get us down.
So look up today and be of good cheer.
An angel of the Lord may be very near.
Letting us know when Gabriel blows that last trumpet sound.
We'll be in Heaven with angels all around.

Thou My God

Thou my God art mighty God indeed.
One that answers every prayer and supplies every need.
A God who has raised the dead and parted the sea.
A God who will fight and win every battle for me.
Thou my God are merciful and kind.
One of mighty strength who can even heal the blind,
An armor and shield thou my God shall be.
When troubles and trials try to take away my victory.
So I look up and behold that thou art the mighty lamb.
Who will someday take me to the blessed promised land.
Thou my God art a mighty God indeed.
I put my trust in thee and only on thee will I believe.

Spring

The warm breeze flows gently through the air.
Springtime has arrived to these mountains so fair.
Dormant trees spring forth with buds of new life.
To the eyes of the beholder, it's a beautiful sight.
Tiny squirrels are scampering from tree to tree.
In the distance, a cluster of robins you can see.
The beautiful flowers will bloom upon the hills.
Among them are roses, lilacs, and daffodils.
The fields that were once dormant at last will turn green.
Winter has passed, and now it is spring.
Although the arrival of spring will soon unfold.
These West Virginia mountains hold beauty that can never be told.

Lord I Need Your Touch Today

Lord, I need your touch today.
To help me and strengthen me along this way.
I am so weak but thou Lord art so strong.
Take me as I am, Lord, for to you I belong.
From the dust of the earth my body was made.
Life was given to me from my mother's womb as a babe.
From the depths of my heart, I cry unto thee.
Asking you, Lord, today to hear my plea.
My troubles seem to be so hard to hear.
I call on you and I know you will hear my prayer.
You, Lord, are a shelter from the storms of this life.
Today please deliver me from my troubles and strife.
Everything I ask is all in your name.
Trusting in you, Lord, for you will always be the same.
You are a true friend that sticketh closer than a brother.
I will trust you, Lord, for without you, there is none other.
So take me and shield me from all the strife.
I'll be safe in your arms from the troubles of this life.

Walk On

Walk on, my friend, although the burden is hard to bear.
Trust in the Lord, and He will answer your prayer.
Walk on…when the day is long.
The Lord will put in your heart a new song,
Walk on…when everyone else is gone.
The Lord has promised you will never be alone.
Walk on…when the pathway looks dim.
The Lord sticketh closer than any friend.
Walk on…for soon the dark clouds will fade away.
The Lord has promised us a brighter day.
Walk on…and upon the Lord, cast all of your care.
He has promised that He will always be there.
Walk on, my friend, walk on down the road.
Soon the Lord will take us to our Heavenly abode.

Praise

Lord, I want to give you praise today.

For helping me and guiding me along this way.

Praise, honor, and glory belong only to you.

You are a faithful friend who is loving, kind, and true.

The earth and everything within was made by your hands.

As in the beginning, it was part of your plans.

Lord, I praise you and lift up your name today.

For your strength and guidance along the way.

There were times when I thought I couldn't go on.

Then I heard you whisper, "Child, you are not alone.

I'll always be there when your load is hard to bear.

You can cast upon me your burdens and every little care."

Lord, I want to praise your Holy Name.

You are a true friend who'll always remain the same.

Lord, I Depend On You Each Day

Each day I listen to your voice.

Guiding me to make the right choice.

You are a friend who'll be there till the end.

I know on you, Lord, only can I depend.

To guide me safely along the way.

Teaching me to depend on you from day to day.

When it seems that I am in despair.

On you, Lord, I cast all my care.

I know when I reach Heaven some day,

I'll be glad I trusted you to guide my way.

Lord, I Long To Be With You

Lord, I long to be with you.

In Heaven where all things will be brand new.

A place to lay my burdens down.

To receive a robe of white and a shining crown.

Where there'll be no sorrow or pain to bear.

Never a heartache or never a care.

A new name will be given unto me.

For at last my spirit will be set free.

Lord, I long to be with you.

I'll wait patiently until my work on earth is through.

Sometimes my trials are hard to face.

I look unto you, and you will give to me more grace.

Grace that's sufficient and each day made anew.

Until I can be in Heaven with you.

Grace

God's grace is sufficient to meet my every need.
I call upon His name and on Him I will believe.
That He will give me grace to be able to stand.
Until I can reach that blessed promised land.
Where my sorrows and tears will all be past.
For I'll be safe at home in Heaven at last.
Heaven will be a beautiful place.
I will enter the gates just a sinner saved by grace.
Sometimes my trials are so hard to bear.
He whispers, "Trust me, child, and cast upon me your care.
My load was heavy when I died upon the cross.
I gave my life completely to save all the lost.
Today, my grace is sufficient to help you stand.
Until I can take you to that blessed promised land."

The Presence Of Someone Near

One day I felt the presence of someone near.
When I turned around to look, the image disappeared.
God promised in His word that He would always be there.
To comfort and help us when we call on Him in prayer.
There's not a problem too big or a problem to small.
God can solve them all if on Him we will call.
I put my faith in God from day to day.
He touches me and takes my burdens away.
There's not a doubt in my mind the image was God that day.
Letting me know He'll always be there to guide my way.